PEACH, LIMESTONE, AND GREEN

Letters and Poems through Loss and Grief

Jerry R. O'Neill

WESTBOW PRESS
A DIVISION OF THOMAS NELSON
& ZONDERVAN

Copyright © 2015 Jerry R. O'Neill.

All rights reserved. No part of this book may be used or reproduced by any means, graphic, electronic, or mechanical, including photocopying, recording, taping or by any information storage retrieval system without the written permission of the publisher except in the case of brief quotations embodied in critical articles and reviews.

WestBow Press books may be ordered through booksellers or by contacting:

WestBow Press
A Division of Thomas Nelson & Zondervan
1663 Liberty Drive
Bloomington, IN 47403
www.westbowpress.com
1 (866) 928-1240

Because of the dynamic nature of the Internet, any web addresses or links contained in this book may have changed since publication and may no longer be valid. The views expressed in this work are solely those of the author and do not necessarily reflect the views of the publisher, and the publisher hereby disclaims any responsibility for them.

Any people depicted in stock imagery provided by Thinkstock are models, and such images are being used for illustrative purposes only. Certain stock imagery © Thinkstock.

ISBN: 978-1-4908-8239-0 (sc)
ISBN: 978-1-4908-8240-6 (e)

Library of Congress Control Number: 2015908646

Print information available on the last page.

WestBow Press rev. date: 06/04/2015

Contents

Foreword xi
Preface xiii

Peach 1

Letters

Letter # 1 5
Letter # 2 8
Letter # 3 10
Letter # 4 13
Letter # 5 15
Letter # 6 17
Letter # 7 19
Letter # 8 21
Letter # 9 23
Letter # 10 25

Poems

Born! 29
Sarah 30
Call of the Orchard 31
Another Orchard 32
Walk in the Orchard 33
Sister Wisdom 34
Safe in the Rain 35
Tender Knowing 37
Absorbed 38
Sacred Silence 39

Ordained Beams Shining	40
Stony Ridge	41
Erie	43
Flow River Flow	45
Invited to Dance	46
Eyeful Ear	47
Again	48
Gleam	49
Held	50
Heart of God's Apple	51
By walking	53
First Kiss	54
A Wedding	55
In the Warm Face of Sunrise	56

Limestone 57

Letters

Letter # 11	61
Letter # 12	63
Letter # 13	65
Letter # 14	67
Letter # 15	69
Letter # 16	71
Letter # 17	72
Letter # 18	74

Poems

Dubuque	79
Limestone Road	81
Limestone	82
Tiny Sprig	83
My Shadow Crow	84
Spirit of Home	85
Socked In	86

November 1st	87
Melancholy Gift	88
At Table with Grief	89
Through Purple Door	90
New Year	91
Light of Night	92
Night Rain	93
Faint Heart Beat	94
A Stone	95
Phone Call	96
How Am I Not?	97
In Dead of Night	98
Surprised by Silence	99
Lighthouse Litany	100
In Numb of Winter	101
Love Embodied	102
In the Moment	103
Yearning	104
What if?	105
Friendship	106
Bare and Still	107
Unknowing	109
Celtic Cross	110
Fearsome Canyon	111
Crack in the Door	112
Even on Shortest of Days	113
On this September 11th	114
One White Rose	115
Pining for Church	116

Green 117

Letters

Letter # 19	121
Letter # 20	123

Letter # 21 125
Letter # 22 127
Letter # 23 129
Letter # 24 131

Poems

Fresh Green Leaves..135
Now Comes the Poet 136
Sacred Cedar... 137
Visitor 138
By a Sea of Grace 139
The Dreamer in Me Asks 140
New Wings..141
Dawn of Pentecost 142
Evergreen Island... 143
Outside Worship 144
Her Smile.. 145
All Saints' Sunday 146
Wave of Brightening.. 148
Wet Whidbey Dawn 149
Holmes Harbor 150
Sound of Trains.. 151
Thanksgiving.. 153
Katie Next Door 154
Sensing Her Nearness... 155
Whidbey Green... 156
Blessed Assurance... 158

Acknowledgements...159

*Our grief
is a journey
that knows its way*

***

*A book is a path of words
which takes the heart
in new directions.*

John O'Donohue

Foreword

Jerry O'Neill is a friend, a colleague, and a fellow traveler on this spiritual journey we call life. Through his letters and his poetry, Jerry faces many of the struggles and joys that he has collected along the way. Through his writing he learned to see life with new eyes and in a newer dimension. From the cold, harsh reality of tragic grief forced upon him and the harness of a stone to the sweet taste of a sunrise and the dawn of a new life, Jerry carries us through his path and helps us to see life in a new way.

It was my privilege to officiate at Jerry and Carol's wedding a few months ago. It was a joy to witness Jerry's growth through his grief to the point where he was able to share his life and love again. As I watched them distribute Communion to their friends and family, I realized the healing power and growth that can come through grief. May you also know this power and may this little book of wisdom aid you in this walk.

Through your reading of his journey may you come to discover the tender heart and healing balm that lies within this man and expressed through his writing as he travels from Peach, to Limestone, to the Green that we share.

Chaplain Dave Bieniek
Hospice of Whidbey General Hospital
Whidbey Island, WA
March 17, 2015

Preface

Morning has arrived and once again blessed by quiet time for devotions I take a walk with Mellie through the towering green Cedar and Douglas Spruce here on Whidbey Island. For the past five years I have been on a contemplative journey through loss and grief, time and again discovering beauty in both bright and dark places, most surprised at the tasty fruit melancholy brings.

The letters and poems included in this book have not been written for literary merit but as a spiritual exercise. With my heart broke wide open by the sudden death of my wife, I have leaned into and followed the promptings of grief. Gazing over inner and outer landscapes I have searched my origins, let go of old realities, and made room for new life to emerge. Peach, limestone and green have been the metaphors that have shaped this collection and helped me express the creativity and profound sense of unity I have experienced along the way. Furthermore, *peach* connects me with the fruit orchards near Crozet, Virginia where my father was born and raised. My wife Denise and I grew up in Dubuque, Iowa on the *limestone* bluffs along the Mississippi River. And the year-around *green* of the Pacific Northwest symbolizes so well the new life I see emerging for me on Whidbey Island.

Writing letters to family and friends, especially those I wrote to Annie, a childhood friend who resurfaced in my life right at the time of Denise's death, has brought comfort and insight while navigating through the most difficult stages of my grief. Writing poems allowed the gentle flow of Spirit to bring hope and healing beyond the confines of logic and the limits of my understanding.

Writing has been like the orchard keeper riding on his tractor. I have fixed my eyes on the fruit trees entrusted to me, reflecting on how I best spade the soil, prune, plant, and harvest the sacred fruits of life. In the process I have gained a sense of who I am, where and to whom I belong. Every day with Spirit kindling the darkness of my loss and grief, writing words on a page has helped me connect to inner truth, helping pave the way for the next chapter in my life.

Offering these letters and poems in gratitude, I pray that the seeds of wisdom and hope they contain take root, a gentle rain of grace seeps through layers of life into the soul, and that a glimmer of green shines through.

PEACH

I have tasted faith
known the fertile humus
of soul's dark winter
and I have tarried

...for another orchard
at least I hope there is
the fruits of which
promise to satisfy fully

Letters

Letter # 1

DENISE (PETERS) O'NEILL
March 31, 1952-February 16, 2010

February 28, 2010
Champlin, Minnesota

Dear Family and Friends,

Your many thoughts and prayers lay on my broken heart. In time I trust they will begin to sink in and help me heal. Until then I simply want to say thanks to you for your kind words, for sharing your memories of Denise with me and others and for reminding me of your continued friendship.

By the messages I have read on Facebook I gather few of you know many details of Denise's sudden and unexpected death. I hope this letter may be of some help:

After spending a particularly pleasant extended St. Valentine's Day weekend together we began Tuesday, February 16 as usual. We had coffee together and went on our early morning walk. We showered, dressed and I kissed Denise as she went off to school for a day of teaching at Washington Elementary in Anoka. There was no hint whatsoever of any threat to her health. Fifteen minutes later I received a call from the school. Denise had come into the building and gone straight to the copying room. As she stood by the copier she suddenly become dizzy and collapsed. A colleague caught her and gently lowered her to the floor. Within minutes paramedics were at her side working to revive her. Her heart had completely stopped.

Upon arriving by ambulance Denise was taken to the heart center at Mercy Hospital in Coon Rapids. When I arrived a few minutes later a chaplain met me at the door of the ER and asked me to sit with her. She told me

Denise had suffered serious heart failure and that I could expect word from a cardiologist before long. Minutes later, called to the ICU, a doctor told me preliminary tests revealed a perfectly healthy heart and arteries with no apparent heart damage. He was cautiously optimistic, their team having stabilized her. However, for reasons they would soon discover, her heart was still not beating properly.

Less than an hour later a neurosurgeon and his medical team joined my daughters Toby and Brooke and me together with a circle of friends, many of them teachers from Denise's school as well as her principal. The doctor explained to us that further testing showed Denise had suffered a stroke due to an aneurysm in her brain. The immediate damage was devastating with little of her brain left functioning except a few basic reflexes.

After collecting ourselves we went to Denise's bed side. A prayer shawl was placed across her chest as she lay peacefully, angelically. For two hours we prayed and said our goodbyes. Then at a few minutes past 1 p.m., Tuesday, February 16th our beloved Denise quietly slipped away.

As you can imagine, what with her amazing health and vitality, the depth and breadth of our relationship and the sudden, totally unexpected nature of her death, we have all been swept away in a sea of emotion and a flurry of activity. Love from all over the country and around the world has been pouring out upon us as we have trudged through the necessary steps for closure.

I can't begin to explain the depth of my grief or suggest how long I will be incapacitated. I do know the faith and school communities have been amazing and God's grace more amazing still. Denise's funeral last Saturday, February 20th at Cross of Glory Lutheran Church, Brooklyn Center, was filled to overflowing with people (lots of children) laughter, words of hope and stirring music. In true Denise spirit, we literally danced in our pews and down the aisle as we left the sanctuary with the song "Oh, Ancient of Days!"

On Monday, February 22, a small group of family and friends met in the Lakewood Cemetery Chapel near what was Denise's and my favorite city lake area of Minneapolis. After a brief moment of silence we sang "Children of the Heavenly Father", prayed and went for our vehicles to proceed to the gravesite. We laid Denise's remains in the "Garden of Serenity" next to a lovely lake and a host of flower beds soon to burst forth this spring with thousands of red and yellow tulips.

In the days and weeks to come I plan to write and travel, visiting people who were not able to be with us at the time of Denise's funeral. I will take a leave of absence from work long enough to allow this sea change to subside and a new landscape come into view. I feel surrounded by the love and care of so many. I know I will not journey alone. What's more, the presence of my soul mate is now felt and experienced in a new and even more profound way than the 42 years I was blessed to know and love Denise in the flesh.

Stirred by the Spirit of our Creator, moved by God's love in the Word made flesh, and enlivened by news of Jesus' resurrection a mantra has now come to me and is often upon my lips, "No Shame! No Worries! Great Joy!"

Again, I thank you. The days ahead will be made easier, our hearts comforted by so many who care, showering us love, hugs and kisses. May God bless our memories of Denise Peters O'Neill and may we have many occasions to enjoy sharing those precious memories with each other in the months and years to come.

In God's love,

Jerry

Letter # 2

March 3, 2010
Champlin, Minnesota

Dear Annie,

Family and friends will gather at Denise's gravesite in Lakewood Cemetery tomorrow to celebrate what would have been her 58th birthday. In what promises to be a sweet sadness I will strap on my guitar and lead the group in a number of songs we've enjoyed singing together over the years.

There was no singing at a cemetery just outside Charlottesville, Virginia at this same time twenty years ago. There huddled under a tent I broke an edgy silence with words of love and appreciation for my Uncle Frank. It was Frank, my Dad's next older brother, who intervened the fall following my graduation from high school and helped bring about a dramatic change in the course of my life.

I had dropped out of college and spent the rest of my student loan on a train ticket to Seattle. There I worked selling shoes on University Avenue not far from the Huskies' stadium. I wanted to enroll in school again, but not being a resident in the state of Washington either disqualified me or made tuition costs prohibitive. One place seemed especially inviting. A counselor from Seattle University, a Catholic Jesuit school, said they would accept me for the winter term if I could swing it financially. A part-time job selling shoes was not going to cut it. So, I returned to my parents' place in Dubuque that Christmas prepared to sign on with the Marines and a tour to the war zone in Vietnam just like my brother Gary and so many others ended up doing.

That's when I got a call from my Uncle. In his smooth, Virginian accent Frank said, "Jerry, I understand you're planning to go into the military. I would certainly respect your decision were you to do that. However, I have deep concerns about the war in Vietnam and the likelihood of your going there. Is there a school you would like to attend realizing you could join the military a little later if that was your choice? I said, "Uncle Frank, I would like to attend Seattle University and they have said they would accept me." "Jerry," Frank replied, "If you'd permit me, I would like to give you the money you need to go to school and get a degree." I gladly accepted.

How the enormous love and generosity that ran through my Uncle Frank's veins gave way to deep, dark depression I'll never know this side of God's Kingdom. But perhaps a reopened wound of enormous grief from his family of origin is what led Frank on this very day two decades ago to desperately flee to the top of a mountain, grip a firearm, point it at himself and pull the trigger.

I lost more than a generous uncle that spring day in the Blue Ridge Mountains. I lost a family dream. All of us thought Frank would help the family rise above the tremendous loss of my Grandfather John when my dad was only four and Frank was just six years old. Grandmother Mary became bedridden shortly after Grandpa's death with a crippling mental illness and died when Dad was thirteen. And if that wasn't enough injury in one generation, the family peach and apple orchards and their beautiful brick colonial home were lost in the Great Depression.

A wise Irish poet suggests that what seems dark, destructive and forlorn might actually be a destiny that looks different from inside the eternal script. From the Holy Book we are assured "treasures of darkness, the hidden riches of secret places" (Isaiah 45:3). Will loss become for me a holy place where by grace I will receive with courage and compassion signs of new life, clarity of the person I really am, a peek at my hidden wholeness, a glimpse of my true place of belonging? Time will tell. But for now I take comfort in knowing Denise, my dad who died some years ago, and my Uncle Frank have all entered the beauty of eternal tranquility, a place where there is no more sorrow, separation, mourning or tears.

I think that will be a nice place for us one day, Annie. What do you think?

Your childhood friend,

Jerry

Letter # 3

March 5, 2010
Champlin, Minnesota

Dear Annie,

Isn't it amazing how some places are like magnets? Platteville, Wisconsin is such a place for me. For starters, I was born in Platteville on a Saturday in the middle of a snow storm. Did I ever tell you that? In fact, my birth was newsworthy. The caption in the Platteville Journal on Thursday, December 21, 1950 read: "Police Help Stork"

On a Friday night, my parents, Madge and Robert O'Neill of Dubuque, arrived in Platteville, too late they thought, to disturb Lloyd and Myrtle Kitto, grandparents on my mother's side. So, they stayed the night in a local motel. What happened next was described this way in the area newspaper: "During the early morning hours the stork fluttered above the room and indicated it was time to keep their appointment at Municipal Hospital. At five o'clock Mr. O'Neill called the taxi, but he could not get an answer. Then a policeman came to the rescue. He loaded the anxious couple into the squad car and took them to the hospital. A short time later—a boy!"

Annie, didn't you have relatives in Platteville? We went there to see my grandparents fairly often throughout my childhood even after you and I had become fast friends. Most of our visits were on a happy note, picnics in the city park near the municipal swimming pool, Main Street parades on the 4th of July, sweets from the candy dish at Aunt Hazel's place. Some trips to Platteville however, were abrupt, scary escapes from Dad's drinking gone wild. It's strange how a place can hold so many memories, and like a battery made in the factory near my grandparents' place, the cells of

Peach, Limestone, and Green

emotion associated with those memories still have a powerful charge, firing on contact.

While I visited Platteville to see my grandparents, Denise traveled to Platteville to visit her Grandma Tatge. Turns out my mother, Madge, and Denise's mother, Donna both grew up in Platteville at about the same time. And long before Mom would express her displeasure with my choice to date Donna's daughter Denise, and later marry this Catholic girl, my mother already held a grudge against Donna's family because Donna's dad allegedly stiffed my grandpa for a set of tires from his gas station, leaving town without paying his bill.

Upon graduating from Dubuque Senior High School in 1969 I enrolled in the same school you did, at the University of Wisconsin, Platteville. Where were you, Annie? What dorm did you live in? I didn't stay on campus. I lived at home and commuted, working at the Lang Ski Boot Company in Dubuque second shift to help foot the bill. Before the first term ended I dropped out of school, took what was left of my school loan and headed for Seattle where the song told me I would find "the bluest skies I'd ever seen."

Didn't you say you lived in Platteville recently until your parents passed? You know my first funeral was in Platteville. Grandma Myrtle was just 64 years old. She died in the same hospital I was born. Older brother Gary and I went up for the service. The only thing I remember about that day with any detail was actually on our way to Platteville. Gary had replaced the hood on his '52 Chevy but had failed to attach it properly at its hinges. On our way down a steep hill just outside Dickeyville the hood lifted up and flew like a kite high up into the air. Looking in his rear view mirror in horror, Gary watched his spendy investment bank to the right and crash into a ditch off the side of the road. I broke out in laughter. Gary could have cried.

Tears from both belly laughs and gut-wrenching sadness have been part of my journey in the wake of Denise's death. I know through tears we are graced with a richer understanding of reality, but dead at 57! We thought Grandma died young! Just 48 hours after we had celebrated Valentine's

Jerry R. O'Neill

Day, Denise's spirit was suddenly lifted, soaring up, out of sight while all I could do was watch in horror as her beautiful body crashed to the ground. Denise's ashes are buried in Minneapolis, in the Garden of Serenity at Lakewood Cemetery. One day, Annie, my remains will be laid beside hers, our Platteville roots at last resting in peace. And we will be, as the saying reads inside our wedding bands, "Together Forever".

Your childhood friend,

Jerry

Letter # 4

March 8, 2010
Champlin, Minnesota

Dear Annie,

Time is suddenly, painfully present in abundance, one twenty-four hour period after another. What utter contrast this is from the days leading up to Denise's death.

Perhaps like you today, I had been accustomed to living the full schedule—meetings, deadlines, community affairs. Denise was a teacher who knew no other way than to pour herself into her work while generously investing in family, friends and home. She was the expert at time management, the queen of multi-tasking, the "white tornado" capable of sucking up and squeezing out meaningful productivity seemingly every waking moment. Denise knew the value of time and together we knew what shortage of time feels like; or so we thought.

Death changed all that in a split second. At the beautiful, vibrant, still young age of 57, in what otherwise appeared to be near perfect health, a time bomb exploded (cerebral hemorrhage) giving shortage of time a whole new meaning.

Oh, how presumptuously we entered each day believing we would travel long and luxuriously well into our years of retirement. But the train stopped a little past 1 p.m. on February 16th and life for me since has felt, on the one hand, like a grossly unfair shortage of time while on the other, just so much dead space, idle time, people, places and things like trees and landscape fast passing by, going this way and that way while I am left feeling like all I have is time.

Jerry R. O'Neill

Pain piled upon pain, I find myself afraid that what I have most of today will chase you and others away, my abundance causing you to distance yourself out of fear, fear of simply not having enough of your own precious time.

Your childhood friend,

Jerry

Letter # 5

Champlin, Minnesota
March 9, 2010

Dear Annie,

When we were kids what did you want to be when you grew up? I remember my Dad being quite concerned that I, unlike him, find a job that would really suit and satisfy me the most. He asked me, "Jerry, what do you want to do when you become a man?" I told me, "I really don't know, Dad. I do know that I want to help people."

Someone has said that if you lose yourself in your work, you will find who you are. This may be true for most people. However, I discovered just a few years ago in the throes of clinical depression that because I was raised in a family where addiction existed, I entered work with a deeply rooted, compulsive need for the approval of others. I discovered much of my work and drive for success over the years were misguided attempts to establish a sense of identity, value and well-being; all desperate striving to restore within me an emotional loss from childhood. Much to my surprise, I had learned to survive loosing myself to please others.

Denise lived through years of this co-dependent behavior asking me time and again why I wasn't satisfied with the wonderful life we had co-created, why I was always looking for the next thing in search of contentment. I'm so glad she lived long enough to learn and understand the powerful addiction that had plagued me for years. And in the same way she gave herself so generously to boldly back me in my work (though she never really liked being married to a pastor) Denise became by far the strongest and most consistent supporter in my recovery.

Annie, you currently face a change in your work. Like me, you seem to favor a job that makes a difference for others. There are probably a number of different kinds of voices calling you to all different kinds of work. The challenge is to find out which is the voice that speaks for the person, by God's grace, you really are. In the wake of Denise's death I too face a change in my work, because even if I return to the job I have had, all of what I knew before will be different now.

So, may we both hear the voice that calls us to that place where, strong in the person God has made us, we can with deep gladness lose ourselves in loving service to others.

Your childhood friend,

Jerry

Letter # 6

Champlin, Minnesota
March 10, 2010

Dear Annie,

I find myself wondering today how Denise would have handled her grief were I to have been the one who died first. Would she have given herself the time I am taking to heal and be restored? Would she have spent the days and weeks I have spent just getting by, leaning on the support of family and friends? With a school full of children eager to learn and an already over-worked staff would she have thought it still right and necessary to take an extended leave from her work as I have? Would she have given herself such permission to grieve?

Oh, I know everyone grieves differently and even if a person returns to a near normal routine one cannot tell for sure on the outside just how much that person is still wounded and crying on the inside. I know when Denise had major surgery years ago she took the time her doctor told her would be necessary to properly heal. (Though you should know she scheduled her surgery during Easter break so she would miss the least number of days off work.) Still no doctor can begin to tell someone how long before their broken heart is healed and on what day they should resume the full gamut of their responsibilities again.

Denise had a high tolerance for pain. In actuality she had a masterful way of putting mind over matter. She seldom permitted herself to let a cut or a strained muscle slow her down. I will never forget how she pushed through the worst phase of her polymyalgia rheumatica, I needing to help her simply crawl out of bed, yet she missed just one half day of school that whole time and that was only because a medical test she had to take could not be scheduled before or after school hours.

Annie, how much time did you take off from your responsibilities upon the death of your first husband? Did you give yourself permission to grieve as long as it would take to allow your heart to fully heal or did you simply gut it out, get back in the saddle and heal on the run? I know there's no sense in comparing since we are wired differently and my circumstances are probably quite different from what yours were. But today I'm just wondering…

Your childhood friend,

Jerry

Letter # 7

Champlin, Minnesota
March 10, 2010

Dear Annie,

I'm thinking of Rose Street Woods not far from your house on Walnut. Of course, that whole area was developed into a dozen or more homes by the time we reached high school. But as a boy it was a wild and mysterious place that invited me in to escape the world I knew and explore a world waiting to be discovered. I climbed trees for a view of Loras College and the bluffs beyond, buried "treasures" in secluded places and the coolest thing was taking into the woods cardboard, blankets, and old lumber and with lots of branches and leaves building my own private fort.

In a fort all my senses came alive. I could smell the dirt and hear the trees sing in the wind. In the confines of that make-shift refuge my imagination soared and though I lost view of the outside world, in this place of solitude I discovered an untold journey into my inner world.

Grief is like Rose Street Woods, drawing me into a wild and mysterious place where everything looks different, where hidden treasures surprise me and where, like a fort confining much of me to death and dying, a whole inner world is opened for me to explore.

In the world of Myers-Briggs, Denise was an ESTJ. She could be intuitive but her obvious strength was sensory, keenly aware of the people, places and things around her. I am an I N F J. To the extent Denise favored the outer world of color, form and hands-on activity; I prefer at least as much the inner world of thought, feeling and faith. Denise encouraged me to cross the threshold and be grounded in the outer world and I encouraged her to let go of her outer world to explore a soulful inner cosmos of beauty and grace.

I noticed on a Facebook entry, Annie, that you are an ENTJ. What world do you prefer? I suppose it depends on your situation. When under duress from loss and grief did you go in or out? Did you step up tending to the people, places and things around you or did you let go and avail yourself to the surprise treasures found in the inner world's unlimited time, space and span of life?

Annie, for all the talk of outer and inner worlds I hope I haven't got us lost in the woods. I'm just trying to integrate and find my way through lessons we are learning on the journey through loss and grief.

Your childhood friend,

Jerry

Letter # 8

Champlin, Minnesota
March 11, 2010

Dear Annie,

Glad you received my book and CDs. Poetry and music have been so important to me in expressing my deepest thoughts and feelings. These have led me to my core and back out again. They expose my pain and brokenness and help me delight in the healing presence of a loving life source.

Denise found expression in the down to earth hands-on activities of a given day. When she set the table for a meal, for example, it was a work of art. Crafts were her preferred creative outlet but done only if what she took time to make was pleasant to the eye, easy on the pocket book and above all useful.

Annie, what has been your creative outlet, your means of soul reflection, your preferred medium for the deepest expression of who you are? When I took up playing guitar and singing in my brother Gary's garage band the summer before sixth grade what did you take up to let your light shine? Where did you go? What from a million possibilities did you choose to bridge your innocent childhood with the turbulence of adolescence and the scary vast sea of adulthood? How have you kept your soul afloat all these years through so many fierce storms of life? What kind of music have you found sooths you? What words mend your heart when it's broken? What disciplines supply you fresh juice when your life goes bone dry?

Jerry R. O'Neill

I suppose its grief stirring up this boatload of searching questions. Thanks for taking time to read and reflect with me. Maybe you'll even share a few questions and answers of your own.

Your childhood friend,

Jerry

Letter # 9

Champlin, Minnesota
March 12, 2010

Dear Annie,

In wisdom from sacred texts we are told that honesty can save our lives. (Proverbs 1:4) A couple days ago I met with a financial advisor to discuss how I will manage without Denise's income. I told her I felt like a wimp grieving so openly and taking so much time to recover. She looked me straight in the eye and said, "Jerry, you would be a wimp were you to deny your grief and return to work too soon and ill-prepared."

The shock of the sudden death of someone as close and so deeply loved as Denise was to me leaves most people numb and unable to feel anything. I knew that numbness for about the first twenty-four hours. After that one wave of excruciating pain after another swept through me leaving me days on end unable to do much of anything.

Thankfully, the work I've done in 12 Step recovery has led me to an honest admission of my powerlessness and an honest acceptance of my responsibility to lean into the grief, reach out to God and others for help, and take the time necessary for the pain to eventually subside and healing to begin. While I could never have sufficiently prepared for this devastating loss, my recovery work has helped me find self-respect and lots of love from the understanding and warm embrace of others. So, I'm happy to tell you, Annie, with friends like you, an amazing family, and my faith community I am blessed with a good and steady supply of these essentials.

But again to be honest, the ache that concerns me most as of late is the agony that has come with the abrupt withdrawal from Denise's physical presence, her touch, her embrace, the intimacy we found so satisfying. I hunger now just to be held by a woman and it scares me to think of how quickly I could invite someone into something we would both likely live to regret.

I hope this honesty does not make you too uncomfortable. It helps knowing you've been through this yourself. A colleague tells me such candor is a good sign that I have sufficient self-awareness to make appropriate decisions. I hope he's right.

Your childhood friend,

Jerry

Letter # 10

Champlin, Minnesota
March 17, 2010

Dear Annie,

What is it about poetry that can stir our souls even when we lack understanding of a poem's verbiage and would be hard pressed to offer a logical explanation for the poet's particular choice of words and their arrangement on the page? What better answer might I have to offer on this St. Patrick's Day than to suggest my love of poetry comes from the Irish blood that flows through me? This is one good reason why I celebrate today my roots from Ireland where the poet ranks second only to a king.

Letters Denise and I sent to each other in the early years of our relationship reveal our use of poetry as a means for expressing the inexpressible nature of our love. Indeed, poetry had its special place dating back to the first days of our courtship when I wrote and sang songs to her. Denise enjoyed most of the poems I wrote throughout the years and she was far and away my greatest supporter in the writing and publishing of <u>Out From the Shadows</u>.

While she related most to her Norwegian and Danish background I'm thinking today that perhaps Denise's appreciation for my poetry came from her fiery Irish great grandmother who loved to drink, smoke and dance. So as much as the Vikings made an impression on the people of Ireland a thousand years ago, I know the Irish have had and continue to make an impact of their own, the poetics of the Denise Peters and Jerry O'Neill marriage being no exception.

Jerry R. O'Neill

You have some Irish blood of your own, Annie. May it flow freely in your veins today and stir you to "live your poem" to the fullest.

Happy St. Patrick's Day!

Your childhood friend,

Jerry

Poems

Born!

What a gift to be born!
To be here today
batch of clay
breath
song
and
Spirit
knowing
whence I came
and where I belong!

Sarah

I read today
from the good book
about the surprising birth of mirth,
about the crazy ways of people
that often weigh us down
and the amazing ways of Love
that cannot be explained,
how my world and God's
overlap again this day
and how faith's mystery of enjoyment
forever gifts me with a laugh

Call of the Orchard

I turn the face of my
dawn devotions
toward the orchardist
whose call prompts
a harvest of prayers
placed in the
hungry basket
of my soul

Is this time to move
from make believe
to land secured and
apple trees planted,
or do I settle for fantasy
and feed on the fruit
of an inner landscape
already in my hands?

I turn the face of my
dawn devotions
toward an earthly goal,
and with long loving look
I listen
for wisdom of the wood
and the orchardist
who calls my name

Another Orchard

I have loved deeply
Tasted life at its best
Known the orchard
And now the empty branch

I have tasted faith
Known the fertile humus
of soul's dark winter
and I have tarried

...for another orchard
At least I hope there is
The fruits of which
promise to satisfy fully

Today I walk a dusty path
Drawn by the sight of a bare tree,
the remembered scent of spring blossoms
and a sweet foretaste of harvest

Walk in the Orchard

I want to walk in the orchard
and have you as a companion,
as my grandfather did before me.

So you can softly encourage
and help me avoid the stones
that trip me when I'm alone.

I need to hear the birds sing
together with your voice
stirring my heart to rejoice and give thanks;

To dance with you among the trees
with incense of apple and peach
rising to the heavens!

And to see your smile
as the sun touches the blossoms and the flowers
and makes their faces laugh.

Yes, I can't walk alone in the orchard.
I need you at my side
just as my grandfather did before me.

A rework of Robert Wicks' "The Garden" in memory of John A. O'Neill

Sister Wisdom

Sister Wisdom
came visiting today

In word-free gentleness
we tenderly embraced
Her divine power
like pure, clear waters
flowed through me,
animating my clay
with love and kindness

From her come
reflections of
my hidden wholeness
with wave upon wave
of providence for all

She reveals the rock
wherein my beauty lies,
that holy ground
from which I'm blessed

Her gift to me
that inner strength
of I Am and It-Shall-Be!

Safe in the Rain

She came out
in the rain this morning,
gently, meekly, meandering
into the front yard,
into my sight
through a window
where I kneel to pray

Had it been a sunny day
I would not have enjoyed
this sweet encounter
Hilde, my neighbor's dog
would surely have
chased her away
But man's best friend
had taken shelter
from the rain
leaving the little deer
free to explore
the deep, lush green
of dawn

So it is
with soul
of a broken heart,
held in the hand
of the Maker,
shy as ever,
a part of me
cautious,

Jerry R. O'Neill

        refusing to
        come out into
        the open
        were it not for
        tears and a
        melancholy overcast
        providing
        safe place
        to wander and graze

Tender Knowing

Beyond words
past noise and glare of
pomp and party
a moment...

when love of father and child
shines through,
time crystallized,
gaze giving way
to a hidden presence
of a deepest...
        most tender knowing

Absorbed

Watering flowers
in early morning light
soil gladly absorbs
becoming breakfast
moist and nutritious
to the root

Morning devotions
living water and word
seeps beyond hard mind
into heart opened
moist and nutritious
to the soul

Sacred Silence

Oh Sacred Silence,
be the music I long to hear
the eloquence I seek to speak
a light for simple sight

Gladden my soul's tongue with taste
sweet, fresh and clean

Swirl and soar
like incense
embracing me heavenward
in holy arms of love

Ordained Beams Shining

All
we
ordained
    DNA
        beams
            shining

from soul to sun dial,
interrelated packages
of earthened energy
moving,
    moving,
        moving

not merely in time
nor deep in soul
but in life-giving
fruit-bearing
divine and human
    intercourse

Like sun and rain
on fertile soil
we are lively interplay
of body,
    mind,
        and spirit

with both
pain and
pleasure
in a now
    and eternal
        promise

Stony Ridge

Below the blue hues of mountain edge
and countless evergreen
lies the red soil of stony ridge
the saddest place I've ever been

Where once lush peaches rich and plump
grew in the mountain sun
and red brick house where six boys jumped
Was home for family fun

But sad their daddy's early death
red horseman's evil ploy
and their mother's weak mind and breath
Left little to enjoy

Down went the family's livelihood
Up went their house for sale
Off went the boys where er' they could
Some sold their life to ale

Red soil on white clouds paint lost blood
fire for life a flicker
dreams stream into sorrowful flood
hope wanes for these peach pickers

Years later on this soil he stood
bright shining as a son
He rose above the gloomy wood
seemed like he'd finally won

Jerry R. O'Neill

No! No! Not the scarlet horseman!
amidst the evergreen
blues his mighty weapon
he steals what might have been

Below the blue hues of mountain edge
and countless evergreen
lies the red soil of stony ridge
the saddest place I've ever been

Erie

Erie flows north with brief divide
they merge as one river
casting beyond New York's Grand Isle
a sight that makes hearts quiver

Two figures in wedding attire
pose front this cataract
like waterfall mist drifting higher
soaked in their marriage act
Eyes future set on merriment
from rock their dreams now soar!
So young to face wildlife's movement
backs to its mighty roar

But what's that cloud of vast gray spray
like a prophetess' words
Spelling hardship and dreary days
life cut short, hardly heard
Over symbol of permanence
spills dark side of soul
sweetness swept from their elegance
into sea dark as coal

Who has harnessed these young lovers
elemental motion?
What force field was left uncovered
pouring out death potions?
Aren't Spirit-fed springs and river
beyond this waterfall?
Still this couple quickly withers

Jerry R. O'Neill

                        downcast their curtain call

                Erie flows north with brief divide
                       they merge as one river
        casting beyond New York's Grand Isle
                a sight that makes hearts quiver

Flow River Flow

Flow river flow
Out
      of   control

This the means
to peace and joy,
this the way
of girl and boy

Tears with fears
engulfed by the sea
lives at last
taken seriously

Flow river flow
this be for me
current of grace,
humility

Invited to Dance

Invited to dance
while on my knees
a thankfulness
on my tongue

Like an Irish river tap
Spirit kicked heals
to the ceiling
and
through the roof!

Out the window of
a quiet morning prayer
shown the glow of
wonder and awe
in a friendship
found
and
celebrated!

Eyeful Ear

I am Eyeful Ear
seeing through
what I hear

Hearing what spoke
the world
into being

Being by
the sonic boom
that rolled the stone
from ancient tomb

Again

It happened again!
Loved right into
a brand new day!

Gleam

I laid out this morning
my personal blue-print
In vast stillness
while duty danced
with aspiration,
there came a
sudden storm of generosity
and I saw the most important
who and what
in a gleam
that lies within me

Held

It's a simple place
I seek to reside
pat answers
set aside

Where I walk humbly
one hand holding
my questions

while the other is
held in Love's
all-knowing

Heart of God's Apple

Lingering
below a cheery surface
this dark verse:

"Like the English Sparrow
declared useless, a nuisance—
a worm-like voice is burrowing
into the heart of God's apple
and I feel blown by the wind,
hanging by a spindle leg
on a broken branch."

Where do such thoughts come from?
What is one to do when they show up?
The Good Book says
they're not of God

So do I simply look them in the eye
declare them lies,
deem them of no lasting consequence,
having no place
in God's saving grace?

What?
Not so?
Darkness a cradle
for new growth?
Good fruit rising out of clay?

Jerry R. O'Neill

> Say again
> how God's life-giving light shines
> when we dare to look
> into the heart
> of the world's darkest verse

By walking

By walking
I make the road
      one step
            this way

By walking
I make the move
      next step,
            new groove

By walking
I make the man
      Spirit sent
            Soul print
                  one with the Maker

First Kiss

O, boundless breeze of being
Sudden, soft and savory
Blowing my heart wide open

Touch my skin
Breathe out, breathe in
This vast wonder that I am!

Exist?
Oh, yes
by this:

Love's
    first
        kiss!

A Wedding

A wedding today
in a church
near a lake
in Kenmore, Washington

Witnessing
the estate
of marriage
with its
dowry of delights

Encouraged
to grow
mature in a
sense of wonder

Amazed
at Love's
mysterious
depth of meaning

Present
at the heart
of life's daily
round and rhythm

In the Warm Face of Sunrise

In the warm face
of sunrise
divine eagerness
meets soul's desire

Like countenance of the Savior
love and compassion radiate
outshining the cold,
dark world of condemnation

Hope
is quickened
as life lights the way,
gifting us
with wide eyes to see
and glad hearts to shine
the goodness
in all of creation

LIMESTONE

In the mighty river
of loss and grief
memories settle,
bits in the greater
base of life

Letters

Letter # 11

March 19, 2010
Champlin, Minnesota

Dear Annie,

Piles of papers surround me this morning. My cherry wood desk top usually kept tidy and clean has been flooded by bills, cards and letters, an overwhelming torrent of both heartfelt concern and heartless demand for accountability.

Closest to me in bright red and blue is a ticket that just surfaced from all the stacks. I found it on the windshield of my car the morning after I signed a release at the hospital allowing the mortician to take my wife's lifeless body to the morgue. A drove of vehicles had converged upon my driveway minutes after we left the medical center. I don't remember who drove my car; I don't remember how I got home. I only know that whoever was behind the wheel of my Ford Focus came to the top of our hill and finding no room chose to park on the street. Sometime after two in the morning while I lay in bed begging God to wake me from this horrible dream a law officer stepped out of his squad car and dutifully slapped a $42 fine on my economy compact and then simply drove away.

A friend will work with me in my office again today to help me navigate, sort out and prioritize amidst screaming sheets of paper, receipts and tumbling towers of picture albums, life insurance policies and my estate portfolio. We are both grieving, yet John has always been more clear-headed in matters of finance and so I take comfort in believing he will work with me until this flood of unusual activity begins to subside.

Jerry R. O'Neill

We share, Dear Friend, a wonderful truth; that salvation is a free gift, thanks be to Jesus, our Savior and Lord! What a stark contrast this Good News is before the harsh, bone chilling reality I face again today.

Your childhood friend,

Jerry

Letter # 12

March 20, 2010
Champlin, Minnesota

Dear Annie,

Yesterday I was clearing out one of Denise's drawers next to our bed. Denise was a pitcher; she didn't hang on to things unless they had aesthetic value or practical use. To my surprise I found a number of little things she had hidden away.

There was a pair of wings she wore on her uniform when she was a flight attendant for Northwest Airlines, a few coins she kept from foreign travel and several sweet pins—two with winter scenes, a pretty pink and gold Easter egg, and one a student of hers had made and given her with tiny ginger bread men glued on a shiny platter. She had a few simple Norwegian jewelry pieces that had also been given to her (she never wanted me to spend our money on jewelry for her), and then there was one more thing...a set of booties given to her at birth, her first pair of shoes adorning those tiny feet of hers the day she was taken home from Dubuque's Xavier Hospital in the spring of 1952.

Do you remember the summer just ten years later when you and I went downtown and purchased a pair of white booties at Kresge's as a present for my baby sister, Peggy? I was so excited about finally having a sister and those booties seemed the perfect gift. What followed immediately after that purchase is far less clear in my mind. What I do remember is that upon returning home I found my father passed out on the dining room floor, stone drunk.

A day later Dad took the booties with him in the car to deliver them to Mom and Peggy (kids weren't allowed to visit in hospitals at that time).

Jerry R. O'Neill

Dad never made it to Mercy Hospital. Under the influence of a week of heavy drinking, he had a head-on collision driving up Dodge Street, landing him in jail and those precious booties strewn on a floor mat near the front passenger seat—the car totaled and towed to a local gas station.

Annie, you were such a ray of sunshine! You suggested we be good kids and clean the house. We even waxed the floor which my Mom later said was several layers thick. Then together we took a city bus and got off at the foot of Dodge Street. We proceeded to walk up that busy, bustling highway looking for a banged up '56 Buick. On the south side of the road near the street we would later walk up to reach the hospital, we found the car and retrieved the package of booties with tiny matching "girlie" socks still in tack. Thanks to your help my sister Peggy got her little booties though I'm not sure she knows today all that went into delivering them to her.

A pair of empty shoes by a bed is a symbol of death. To me, however, the booties Denise kept safely hidden away by our bed speak more to the life she lived than the death that took her away. From the day she was born Denise lived with both feet on the ground, moving most of the time. And while I must take baby steps through this grieving process, in true Denise fashion, she took one bold step upon her death landing her safely in the arms of the Savior.

Your childhood friend,

Jerry

Letter # 13

March 21, 2010
Champlin, Minnesota

Dear Annie,

I write to you today full of anger. The weather is beautiful outside, perfect for the walk Denise and I loved to take each morning but Denise is gone and I must walk alone. Stepping out the front door unto the trails of Elm Creek Preserve I find myself yelling at the top of my lungs, chasing the birds away with all my furry.

This is not the way we planned it! Denise was to follow in her mother's footsteps, healthy and strong, sky diving at 80. I don't want to be a single adult. I have not known adulthood without Denise. She and I were in love at sixteen, upon graduating from high school we were on a course for marriage. On our wedding day I was only twenty, she was just nineteen.

I feel angry but I can't really tell the difference between anger and my fears. How will I alone meet the rigors of my work, keep the home up, see that the bills are paid, and do the thoughtful, timely things Denise helped make sure we did for family, friends and so many others? How will I go day in and day out, month after month indefinitely without the love and affection she provided so often and so tenderly? How will I ever find such love and companionship like that again, and were I fortunate enough to find someone, how will I dig up the courage to love like that again knowing how quickly it can all be stripped away?

Do you feel angry sometimes, Annie married not once but twice, yet both men gone and you left single? Do you have fears—job on the line nearing sixty, grandson to raise, and other responsibilities piled to the ceiling? Do

Jerry R. O'Neill

you wonder how you can stay fully alive without a loving companion yet fear the risks of falling in love again?

What are we to do with anger and our fears? I know our faith provides us all the right answers but Annie, I'm even angry at God!

Your childhood friend,

Jerry

Letter # 14

March 23, 2010
Champlin, Minnesota

Dear Annie,

I ran across two things yesterday that brought back Denise's death with painful clarity—a toothbrush and a pill box. The compartments in the box were empty of pills through Tuesday with tablets still in the one marked Wednesday. These were little reminders of something too big for me to handle alone. I had to leave the house and find some company.

Both tooth brush and pill box speak of the daily care Denise took to stay alive and well. They point to the many things we do in an effort to live healthy, productive lives. Yet, in reality, our best efforts can be swept away in the blink of an eye.

For all the reminders of death in my journey through grief I know there are equally as many signs of life able to stir up inside me the waves of eternal time. I do long to bask in that supreme joy that echoes in hearts that beat for God; that joy felt in the warmth of a spring sunrise and is heard in the song of a robin.

Annie, how long did it take after your husband died for you to be moved more by signs of life than death? Others who have experienced life's end for one close to them tell me it depends on the individual and because Denise died relatively young and so suddenly it may take me longer.

I'm wondering, with both your parents gone how does the old neighborhood now appear to you? Does it seem more like a dwindling flame in a cold house or does it point to a warm light of love received in childhood and to an infinitely better place awaiting you in heaven? I do find comfort in fond memories. But I know life goes on for us. There are new neighborhoods, people, places and things to enjoy.

I do appreciate your promise to pray for me. Pray that I have faith to venture out in good courage trusting God's hand will guide and support me in the gradual discovery and growth of a purpose and new life yet to unfold.

Your childhood friend,

Jerry

Letter # 15

Champlin, Minnesota
March 24, 2010

Dear Annie,

Were you ever seriously hurt when you were young? I suppose, like me, you had your share of minor injuries. One morning in early summer my older brother, Gary, made himself a bow with a branch and string. For an arrow he found an old, rusty curtain rod from someone's trash barrel. Eager to show me the cool toy he had made, he said, "Look at this, Jerry!" aimed his "arrow" over my head pulled back the string and fired. Unfortunately, the curtain rod had a mind of its own and sailed right into my face gouging a hole in the side of my nose a fraction of an inch below my left eye. Several stitches and my mother's brief fainting spell later, I was back outside playing with little thought to what could have happened had the rod struck my eye instead.

You probably never knew the injury I sustained on my first attempt to come to your house. Again it involved my older brother Gary who, by the way, in spite of these isolated incidents actually was and continues to be a wonderful brother. I followed Gary into the alley that ran from our street to yours. He was heading over to hang out with your brothers. He didn't want his little brother tagging along. So, to discourage me he started to pitch rocks my way. Well, one pretty good size stone landed just above my forehead requiring a couple more stitches. Apparently, that injury proved to be just a minor setback; it wasn't long after I made it all the way to your house on Walnut Street. And as it turned out the boys were older and talked about a lot of things I didn't understand. That's when you showed up and our special friendship was born.

There is risk of being hurt in any relationship of significance. Vulnerability is required, allowing access to our dreams, thoughts, and feelings. I knew I was vulnerable when I fell in love with Denise. Throughout our years together I actually imagined from time to time what it would be like were Denise to be killed in a car accident or by some other freakish calamity. I wondered why I entertained such morbid thoughts and came to realize I was simply trying to protect myself from what would surely be a devastating blow. As it turned out, I was still woefully ill-prepared the day Denise actually died.

People tell me to give myself permission to be wounded, that because I loved so deeply my wound is deep giving me every reason to be weak, non-functioning and somewhat crazy at times. I've even been told that when I hurt most I heal and grow the most, that loss is the sister of discovery, vital to openness though often accompanied by great pain. I'm not sure about all this, Annie. But I do know that the hurt I have felt with Denise's death is more painful than anything else I have ever experienced; and I'm so sorry you have had to experience pain like this yourself.

Your childhood friend,

Jerry

Letter # 16

Champlin, Minnesota
March 25, 2010

Dear Annie,

A colleague took me out for breakfast yesterday. Filling the space between us with his well-intended, light hearted monologue, I found myself, ears muted, tasteless food in my mouth, longing for eyes, loving eyes that would invite me into real comfort and joy. Have you noticed the softness and gentleness eyes can reveal? When they look at you you feel accepted and affirmed even when, and perhaps especially when, not a word is spoken.

I miss Denise's eyes. All the words we shared in more than forty years together do not hold a candle to a single loving look Denise offered me with her beautiful blue eyes. When we looked into each other's eyes we could live with a kind of abandon because we knew the source of our joy; that inexplicable delight found in sharing true love.

Yes, words are wonderful but eyes are more wonderful still. Oh, how I long for eyes that delight in who I am, that see the path I must travel, and join me in all the joys and sorrows I will meet along the way. No matter how hard one tries, words alone cannot enliven me. Loving eyes are what I need to put wings on my effort to move ahead, healing, empowering, and readying me to accept the joy of life again.

Isn't it amazing, Annie, how God uses the eyes of those who love us to bring us such comfort and joy? I ache today longing to feel that pure and formless energy of Love's gaze upon me once again!

Your childhood friend,

Jerry

Letter # 17

Champlin, Minnesota
March 25, 2010

Dear Annie,

O.K., tell me its grief, not dementia. I have gone to mid-week Lenten services at Central Lutheran for the past few weeks. So why did I forget to go tonight? On a day I can remember in detail what you and I said and did together fifty years ago why do I have a hard time remembering as simple a thing as the password I have used for the past ten years to retrieve my voice messages?

Experts say it's an enzyme released in my body because I am in grief, a chemical that has both a physical and emotional impact on me. I can expect dehydration and muddled thinking, whirling thoughts and rapid change in sleep patterns, eating habits, and social ability. At a time when all I want is to be alone I hunger like crazy for physical touch, dangerously vulnerable, ready (though not willing) to accept practically any woman's offer of intimacy.

So, what am I to do, Annie? You've been in my spot. What did you do? Did you just drink more water, pamper myself, and try to get as much rest as possible? For how long? Then what? Oh yeah, that's another symptom of grief, the mind working over time, trying to plan out the rest of my life when I can't even remember my next appointment or if I took my meds at lunch time an hour ago. I know Denise is gone but the life we shared is so difficult to relinquish and the inner realities of my loss are the hardest to let go.

No, I'm probably not mentally ill, just mentally overloaded which explains why I missed my appointment with God tonight. What's that you say,

Annie—it's temporary, that what I'm experiencing will pass and will pass quicker and easier if I cut myself some slack? You've always been the more sensible one and I suppose you'll be quick to assure me—God understands.

Your childhood friend,

Jerry

Letter # 18

Champlin, Minnesota
March 26, 2010

Dear Annie,

I have the engagement ring and wedding band I gave Denise in a zip-lock plastic baggie. These bring back memories of when Denise and I went by bus in early March, 1971 to the Salishan Lodge on the Oregon costal route. I surprised Denise with the engagement ring the first day we walked on the beach. Her good sense told her that at nineteen she was too young to get married. (She was actually a few days shy of nineteen at the time.) But knowing I had cleaned toilets on all ten floors of my college dormitory for money to buy the ring must have made it next to impossible for her to say "no".

I remember at our wedding back in Dubuque the same year on August 28th, Pastor Johnson talked about a ring in his homily. He said something about it symbolizing unity, wholeness, commitment, authority and he emphasized it most of all as being a sign of what is eternal. He took our wedding bands and pointed out their circular shape suggesting they were an emblem of completion, strength, protection and continuity.

Denise's wedding band was soon fastened to her engagement ring and she wore them both faithfully. Because she kept her hands so busy, her fingers rubbing against everything from rocks and knitting needles to hammers and paint brushes, the bands wore thin and had to be reinforced by a jeweler several times over the span of our 38 years together in marriage; And that my wedding band still looks practically new says more about how hard I've worked my hands relative to Denise than I'm comfortable admitting.

So what do our rings symbolize now that Denise has died? I know I must continue wrestling with the reality that our roles as husband and wife have ended. But it's so hard to render these precious symbols mere sentimental keepsakes! Every time I look at them in this long night of grief I miss being Denise's husband, a role now just history.

Denise was always determined to be a person separate from the roles she filled. She was willing to be Jerry's wife and made efforts (bristling most of the time) to accept the role as pastor's wife. She was daughter, sister, mother, grandmother, friend and teacher. But separate from all of these and other roles, she was always Denise, a wonderfully capable and gifted child of God. And as I look at her wedding ring now vacant I recall words from the ancient book of Isaiah: "Fear not, for I have redeemed you; I have called you by name, you are mine." These words speak truth concerning the monumental change that occurred upon Denise's death. Denise was never mine to keep nor was I ever ultimately hers.

I know, Annie, I'm beginning to sound like a pastor. I'll take this as a sign of my starting to heal, becoming an active participant in a profound, fearful, and awe-inspiring journey through loss and grief. But to you, I will always be…

Your childhood friend,

Jerry

Poems

Dubuque

On a winding road
through a thousand acres
of warm early autumn color
we come upon a monument
along a ledge high above a
Mighty River

The soul of a miner
now long gone
stirs the heart of new arrivals
our spirits voiced by the mouth of the Catfish
all eyes on the window
through which he escaped

Amidst the weight of lead
and the soaring eagle
he bridged the great divide
between Mesquakie Red Fox
and French-Canadian White
sealed by his marriage to Petosa

Jerry R. O'Neill

Did he deny his mortality
when he ventured here
with little more than a dream
or in the face of death
lived with courage
mounted on wings of divine purpose?

How could he know that his life
would give rise
to a thriving city;
that one miner would be
twenty-five thousand
in little more than fifty years?

Small wonder why our intrigue
on this site where his cabin once stood
from a cedar cross to a limestone tower
lies the Julien in each one of us,
that spirit of Dubuque just waiting to be mined
And in the end, a chieftain's burial

Limestone Road

Childlike feet
scamper
on a limestone road
walking
toward innocence
and the lessening of life's load

Restlessness
echos
on pilgram's path
reminding us of home
and the song sung there
on our behalf

Limestone

In the mighty river
of loss and grief
memories settle,
bits in the greater
base of life
over time
lending firm
sign and wonder
in layers
of becoming

Tiny Sprig

Heart cracked open,
a fossil mind in
field of dry bones,
where once I belonged
I live no longer.
From deep in my clay
comes taste of truth,
that what I will lose
has already died.
Deep knowing
of life born
beyond pale cracks
of vacant endurance,
I thirst for courage
a threshold to cross,
alive once more
by the tiny sprig
of soul's desire

My Shadow Crow

With flight of eagle I am humbled,
with call of dove is my peace,
Yet as my shadow
the wise crow flies
and I the broader
in new daylight

Spirit of Home

I have ridden the night
in a yellow caddy
laughed
at harsh mystery
and poignant realities
walked
between
jagged bluffs
on smooth rock
where evergreens
their roots in
pitted limestone
grow straight
and tall

I have viewed the mighty river
through a small
round window
in the attic
of a chapel
and
felt the
Spirit of Home
beyond
the grave
in the company
of a new friend
for Greta

Socked In

Lonely but not alone
The dim, misty morning
seems asleep and indifferent
I know better
The sun does shine
But my feelings
are like this rainy day

I am socked in,
longing for rays
that give life,
for a warm embrace
to feel whole again

Come, Morning Star
Come
Come soon

November 1st

I looked
out my window
on a first November day
There stood the
fruit tree
I planted
last spring
in her memory

…bare branches aglow
      with light of dawn

And I realized
what the poet meant
when he said,
"There is always music
amongst the trees…"[1]

So I looked,
      I listened,
           and I sang
                  a song of thanksgiving

---

[1] Minnie Aumonier

Melancholy Gift

Beauty swings
in lone tree
not in warm ray
or cold gray
but beyond
sensibility

Cloud and rain
rising and refining—
an interplay
of sense
and Spirit,
thought and imagination

This day
gifting
rich melancholy
to a heart
longing
for Love's embrace

At Table with Grief

I'm at table with Grief
Pondering the best guest list
And how we of kin spirit
Will be seated and belong

Of course Irish blood won't be required
But love for lively music will run the veins
And hearts will beat longingly for the
Spiritual wisdom of the Celts

With breaking of bread let poetry invoke blessing
At every level of human life
Cross every threshold
Let a toast be given to the goodness of our Maker!

And though I've lost one dearly loved
Life becoming a strange and lonely night
I will dwell in the company of the Saints
Our eyes on the dawn of happiness

Through Purple Door

I stand before a purple door
in this merry season
of Christmas
Grief has come to visit.
A deep, dark hue of
life-threatening potential
has taken up house and home
prompting me to wonder
how I might be a gracious host,
not knowing the length
of stay this visitor
may choose or
the permanent damage
that may result

Then wisdom whispers,
"Now is the time to extend
care and deep friendship
Grief has come to open you up
imbuing
beauty, grace
and compassion"

So, with
childlike innocence
vulnerable to a
stranger made friend,
I trust Grief
to lead me through
this purple door
of blessings,
new life
waiting
just beyond
the threshold

New Year

When my eyes grow dim
behind a wet, gray window
and the cold wind of loss
cuts to the bone,
pray I remember
this New Year's flock of colors
and rise for the dance
on an isle of delight!

Light of Night

Two
by the fire
only one
in the chair
warmth of the flame
lonely cool
in the air

Gone
is the sight
of her
mega-watt smile
Come light of night
As I weep
for a while

Night Rain

It's raining
in sunny California,
tear drops
in the middle of the night,
bright eyes and tan faces
gone to bed

A heavy cloud has let loose
and a hurting heart
bleeds
it's a gentle rain
falling, calling
on human soil

Softening hard surfaces,
watering new hopes and dreams,
washing away all
but the most tender
in a moonlit tide
of memories

Faint Heart Beat

The sun is down
shadow up
I go the river
fill my cup
The air is eager
music sad
I play the lonely
find what's glad

Rippled waters
wind is up
I face the furry
empty cup
Who's at home?
Who will I meet?
I play guitar
with faint heart beat

A Stone

I've known the power of a single flame,
a candle
lighting up my soul
stilling fear
chasing loneliness away
But a stone?

Yes
prayed over,
blessed
with the love
and compassionate energy
of others
I am surprised
by a single stone
that accompanies me,
flowing with a
mountain size stream
of peace
and pleasure!

Phone Call

Calling
with condolence
no glib promises
but
divine presence

A voice
offering
is but
a trace of grace
to calamity,
a sprinkle of hope
in a toxic mix
of chemistry,
circumstance
and mishap

A
spark
on a
strong wick
lighting up
a mortal moment,
glowing
in the dark

How Am I Not?

I have journeyed
these grief stricken days,
on path
poet Rumi speaks

Where "How are you?"
is glibly asked
while soul pays toll
for lack of listening

In Dead of Night

Oh, that today, tonight
and tomorrow
I be a light
God lets me borrow
That glad sight
in dead of night
that gives chase
to all my sorrow

Surprised by Silence

Silence greeted me
when I came home last night
after a long day on cacophonous seas,
rocked by smack of choppy words
and rushing waves of human clamoring

To my surprise
this silence
I feared once
in the emptiness of my singleness,
gently embraced me
its potion seeping into my soul
leaving me not void but filled,
graced by a soothing sense
of well-being
lingering
into the light
of a new day

Lighthouse Litany

What is it
about a lighthouse
that intrigues us so?
Built to warn, it woos
Strong in storm, it sooths

When vision is lost,
direction confused,
when the very sense of self
seems to simply vanish
a lighthouse sends rays to find us

Each beam a silent mantra
You are not lost!
You are not lost!
You are not lost!

Past jagged rock
and the cold dark bed
of a watery sound
we commune in a
still, soft lighthouse litany
You are not lost!
Yes, I believe!
You are not lost!
I am beloved!
You are not lost!
Now I belong!

In Numb of Winter

See what love
life's Rose has given!
That in the coldest moment
with every step on ice
a fragrant voice still sings
in a sea of smiling faces
and warmth
is felt
from a
welcoming place
even in the
numb of
winter

Love Embodied

I want love
embodied
I want to be
embraced
To bring it in
The way love goes deep
Stirring all my senses

I want the way it blossoms
into a spray
of loving acts
Not left alone in a dark unknown
I want love alive, in reach
Bursting into
being, belonging, becoming

I want love
to lie
and rise up with me
Dancing
in my heart,
on my mind
in every cell of my body!

In the Moment

Stone bench
my portal
along high line of trees
I am
Cultus Bay Spit
grounded
in the constant
of an
ever-changing
tide

Yearning

This Sabbath morn
Inner Voice adorned
I am quieted
by Love's embrace
A tender silence
face to face
Healer of my loving ill
Comforter who holds me still

What if?

What if
all we are
is one
flimsy, cellulose layer
after another,
just juicy lumps
void
of lasting substance?

What if
upon peeling away
folds of
flesh, mind and spirit
there is
not even a lingering
taste or odor?

What if
in the end
not a tear is shed
as tribute
to the grandeur
of our
essence?

Enough
ifs already!
We are
worth
the Maker's
word
no matter
what!

Friendship

Like rain
grief comes
in and out
of season

And today
as have for me,
I stand in wet shadows
with those who grieve

Heart open to share
light for the way-
enduring friendship,
undying love

Bare and Still

Oh, sweet apple tree
where has your life slipped?
Like tide gone out
lush-leafed limbs
and deep red fruit
but bare branch stubble
with decay-looking dull mud moss
the only hint of green
a dried up skeleton
of what you have been

Still you hold me captive
your bare branch beauty
pointing me into the deep
of this quiet season's mystery
your empty limbs
a web in which
I am woven into
a cycle of life
and eternity

How would it be
if you appeared
in my window
chewed up and spit out
by cold winter wind
naked, exposed
in an arrested posture
unable to stir?

Jerry R. O'Neill

>It would be as though
>my heart and hands,
>my mind and feet
>my very soul
>were suddenly untied
>and life was pouring
>back in again!

Unknowing

Keep me from usual
too soon
Come shake my soul
from sleep,
lulled into wanting
old life back,
by the who and the what
deserving
their own sweet
time and space

Move me beyond
what's normal,
to that found in
fearful absence,
dark hole filled by the
wholeness
of unknowing

CELTIC CROSS

Like a
sphere
circling
round
and
round
as faith turns world upside down
falling we rise to highest ground
always
beginning
without
end
all souls
singing
what's
round
the
bend

Fearsome Canyon

Sky wide
      and a mile deep
Granddaddy
      of fearsome canyons

Wind of flute
      Voice of awe
The chill of life lost
      in the fall

Oh, distant Spirit
      Love's breath of time
Come fill this canyon
      'tween her heart
                …and mine

Crack in the Door

O would that
this be
a light-hearted
story
'bout sweet island bunnies,
and flowers
we adore

But this tells of
dark smoke
covering our lightness,
nasty dry winds
on what's insecure,
empty wings of lesser angels
giving rise to sinking hearts,
sharp nerves on dull edge
and the dreadful sound
of a slamming door!

O tell us that tale
of good news
in the end,
ours the longing
for friendship again
how by a crack in the door
we see vast fertile ground
and by hearty rain of grace
a door handle can be found

Even on Shortest of Days

Seven in the morning
with sun
slowly struggling
free of the
catchy Cascades

Among our options
this dawn of fall
embrace less light
for more

Like coin found
in mouth
of Peter's fish
a sight of light
where least expected

Soulful eye to hill
echoes of sacred yes
each night
a la carte bright
even on
shortest of days

On this September 11th

Night having run away
with late summer temps,
I lift my eyes to the hills
above the harbor

In warmth of rising sun
remembering lives lost
grateful for kindling fire
and the vast circle of saintly heat

Come you sun
Light Almighty
grace this place
with bright of day

Set hearts aflame
for those who've died,
and stir love for the lowliest
from one on high

One White Rose

Two
Canadian Geese,
mates pausing on
peak
of nearby roof
looking westward
before going south

A reflection
on glass
covering
one
white rose
And for a brief moment
I feel her next to me

Pining for Church

Not to be the man
who stood up
and walked west
looking for Church
among pine
and mountain peak,
his children saying
sweet things of him
as if he were
dead

Nor
do I choose
to remain in
what was home,
dying amidst
dishes and fancy furniture
as my children
search far and wide
for the same Church
which I forgot

Based on "Sometimes a Man" by Rainer Maria Rilke

GREEN

In a grove of trees
I looked up
into a myriad of
fresh green leaves

Letters

Letter # 19

Champlin, Minnesota
March 27, 2010

Dear Annie,

You have told me how you love the mild winters there in the state of Washington. Aren't they a contrast to the winters we knew as childhood friends in Iowa! Weather in the Northwest especially in February was a total surprise to me my first year in Seattle. Like you, I was accustomed to Jack Frost's long, harsh hold on a Midwest landscape, our only hope come February—a brief winter's thaw, realizing heavy snow was sure to come again in March.

So you can well imagine my delight in the heart of the city to find beautiful rhododendron in full bloom everywhere I looked on Valentine's Day. Washington poet Laureate Ella Higginson had it right nominating the coast rhododendron for the official state flower. What a perfect choice this has proven to be for the people privileged to live in that wonderful Evergreen State.

Denise died just after the Noon hour in a Minnesota February. Outside her hospital room the day was full of sunshine and warmer than usual temperatures. Inside was sudden midnight with a cold like I had never felt before. A five percent chance of recovery the neurosurgeon told us and there we were, completely caught off guard. Like a strong, Canadian clipper, a deadly winter storm had cut through the room. Our only hope, this side of God's kingdom, was for a brief reprieve, an hour or two, all the while realizing death was sure to come.

Like the pink and white lady's slipper, Minnesota's state flower, Denise was a rare find, with unquestionable beauty, well worth the hunt through the bogs and damp woods of more than 38 years of marriage. Today her darkened ash is buried under a blanket of white snow. And Annie, I'm sure this comes as no surprise that I find myself longing for spring now more than ever.

Your childhood friend,

Jerry

Letter # 20

Champlin, Minnesota
March 28, 2010

Dear Annie,

I joined ranks in a festive parade at Center Lutheran Church in downtown Minneapolis yesterday. While steeple bells rang gloriously, echoing off tall buildings up and down the city streets, several hundred of us waved palm branches and streamers, banged on bongos and shook tambourines. Yet, in spite of the sights and sounds of this gala affair I was one step removed, hardly in the spirit, just falling in line as we made our way around the outside of the church building, through the front doors and into the sanctuary. It was Palm Sunday and I felt more the passion than the pageantry.

What season of the church year was it, Annie, the Sunday you took me to a Nativity Catholic Mass on Rose Street and Buena Vista Avenue? I know we didn't wave palm branches but I did find myself falling in line after you as we entered the sanctuary by way of the center aisle. Well versed in church practice, you bent your knee before entering a pew and I tried to genuflect after you as though I knew what I was doing. Then we peered over the pew as the priest led the service, everyone speaking in a language I had never heard before. You told me it was Latin.

Faith has been the strongest and most benevolent tool at our disposal all through the years. I know it can and has been a help in diminishing the sorrow I have felt following Denise's death. But I have to say that I have felt very little joy, the feelings of life's gifts and triumphs out of reach, devotional reading flat and attendance at church services rote, simply going through the motions.

Jerry R. O'Neill

Perhaps this is all I am to do and all I can expect. Maybe this is the time and occasion like that popular poem suggests, when there is only one set of footprints in the sand, my place being the one who rests secure in the arms of the Lord, the Savior carrying me through this time of grief.

Thanks again, Annie, for sharing your faith with me at such an impressionable time in my life. In part because of you, I have faith today that even though the worship services I have attended lately could just as well have been in Latin, my season for mourning will end and a time for clear, bright Easter joy will come to me again.

Your childhood friend,

Jerry

Letter # 21

Champlin, Minnesota
March 31, 2010

Dear Annie,

I boiled a dozen large eggs early this morning in preparation for a visit with my grandchildren and our annual egg coloring party. Denise loved to decorate Easter eggs. In fact, she had a fetish about eggs this time of year. As soon as we had children of our own she made it a non-negotiable tradition in our household to hang brightly colored eggs both inside and out.

In years when Easter came early and it was still cold, hanging all those silly eggs on tree branches with flimsy little ribbons and hands gone numb was a labor of love. My, how all those times so quickly slipped through our fingers! What I would give to have Denise with us again this Easter decorating and hanging eggs on tree branches, as many as her heart desired.

It is Denise's birthday today. She would have been fifty-eight. A psalmist once prayed, "O Lord, help me to see the shortness of life that I may gain wisdom of heart." Amidst sweet memories that fill this bright, sunny day, there is also a sense of transience that casts a shadow on my heart. Denise has suddenly arrived at her last birthday on earth and I am incredulous that that is it; that her life is over!

Eggs are a universal symbol for the mystery of creation. To see an egg is to anticipate life bursting from primordial silence. Today alongside my joy in knowing Denise lives in the Lord forever, I long for assurance that something of value can be harvested from Denise's disappearance.

These letters, Annie, are in large part my effort to create a living permanence. Yet, like you, I too must gradually discover a new identity, gaining a better

Jerry R. O'Neill

sense of who I am no longer married, separate from my spouse. Denise is gone and now one of the weightiest decisions I face is deciding what to do with my life. Perhaps the egg can help keep it simpler, suggesting that like a chick new life will burst forth for me in its own good time.

I trust you and Nathan will be decorating eggs this week. Whatever the occasion, a holiday, birthday, or no day out of the ordinary, I hope you enjoy each precious moment before it simply slips away and memories colored with hope are all you have left to cherish.

Your childhood friend,

Jerry

Letter # 22

Clinton, Washington
December 2011

Dear Annie,

For years household pets have been an important part of my life. Denise encouraged me to bring two beautiful Burmese cats, Shell and Sable, into our lives when I was in the depths of depression seven years ago. Both cats are petite; Sable is the larger of the two weighing in at less than five pounds. They are affectionate creatures finding their way onto my lap whenever I sit for morning devotions, read at other times of the day or occasionally watch some TV.

More than cute, soft and furry, these two creatures have been soul friends along my path through depression and now more recently through loss and grief. They made the journey from Minnesota to Washington without a whimper and have daily warmed my heart in the cold, lonely hours of my transition into new life on Whidbey Island, helping me cope with the inner experience of being lost and the throes of being different.

This morning they must have known I was in special need of attention. Both cats planted themselves on me, warming my body and soul. There is no filling the void left by Denise's passing but the love and affection of those two kitties do sooth me and give me someone at home to love in return.

Annie, your brothers had quite a few pets as I remember. One stands out in my memory, a baby raccoon. That sure was a cute little thing, fed by a tiny doll bottle. It grew quickly, however, and started to bite; so much for trying to domesticate an animal born in the wild.

Jerry R. O'Neill

I suppose your grandson, Nathan, is your little pet now; yet he too is growing up fast. Do you have other darlings in your home—a turtle, gerbil, hamster, cat, dog? As a working woman, raising a grandchild, you may well pass on having any other bodies in your home to look after. Perhaps Nathan is all you need right now to warm your body and soul.

As you know, though questionable, given my small apartment and two mature cats, I recently chose to bring Mellie Maple Whidbey, a Golden Retriever puppy into my home and new life here on the island. While a lot of work, this precious canine companion has quickly become keenly aware of both my grief and new found joy, teaching me to play, prompting me to get out regularly to walk and to explore, her soul touching mine, helping me feel grounded and more fully human again.

Yes, Annie, I have to say, learning how to lovingly and playfully co-exist with my dog and two cats has helped me heal, connect with the natural world around me, and find peace within. Are you sure there isn't another pet in your future? I know for me, there's nothing quite like a sweet pet to stir up the sheer exuberance of being.

Your childhood friend,

Jerry

Letter # 23

July 7, 2012
Spokane, Washington

Dear Annie,

I'm staying in a hotel just outside Spokane, Washington, on the last leg of a move from Minnesota to Whidbey Island, Washington. As you know, after a trial year living on the island I made the decision a few months ago to sell my house in Champlin and establish a smaller, simpler home on Whidbey. While an estate sale relieved me of the bulk of my worldly possessions, I have still managed to hold on to a truckload of things. Hopefully, it will all fit in my apartment.

Ironically, "Minnesota" is painted in bold letters on the side of my U-Haul truck along with a picture of the state that has been my home for the past 30 years and remains home for my daughter Toby, son-in-law Jay and my precious grandsons, TJ and Carter. Truth be told, Denise would never have agreed to leave family behind for a new life out west. I had put that dream to rest a long time ago for that reason alone. So today it does indeed seem strange how Denise's death resurrected my hopes and desires to live in the Pacific Northwest on the beautiful Puget Sound, amidst snowcapped mountains and lush green all through the year.

Thankfully, everyone in my family seems to understand my need to let go. And it seems all the spiritual greats agree: love that does not let go is not real love after all. Yes, and with phone, Skype, and easy travel to the Midwest I will have every opportunity to stay meaningfully connected to my family and friends.

Daring to sell my house and most of my belongings, move to a new location, embark on a fresh and different approach to the care of souls,

Jerry R. O'Neill

I am striving to make room for the Spirit to transform me and empower me to live out God's call on my life in new and exciting ways. Yes, I know there are challenges ahead. Pain comes with so much change. But by the grace of God I intend to make this end a new beginning, trusting I will gradually discover the growth and purpose meant for me in this new chapter of my life.

Thanks for your invite but I won't drive south to visit you in the Tri-Cities; perhaps another time. Simply writing to you, however, has once again been helpful. Eager to get back to my cats, unload and start the new week fresh I remain

Your childhood friend,

Jerry

Letter # 24

Freeland, Washington
October 10, 2014

Dear Annie,

Journeying with me these past five years, thanks to letters, emails and Facebook, you know how wise and fortunate it has been for me to move from Minnesota one month shy of a year after Denise died. For the past four years this lovely place in the Sound and the amazing people who live here have given me beautiful and safe haven to recognize and creatively acknowledge a key life passage; encouraging me to take time to heal, to feel all the varieties of divine presence that accrue here, and to listen inwardly with complete attention until I hear the inner voice calling me forward.

Each life is a mystery. I may never know why Denise went before me. However, that I am here is a huge affirmation; somehow life needed me and wanted me to be. Trusting this primeval acceptance has opened a vast spring of faith within my heart. It has given me courage and renewed confidence for a journey of discovery, creativity and compassion, blessing me with visible signs of invisible grace.

It's so green with promise here on Whidbey Island; new life emerging year around! Of course, welcoming Mellie Maple, a Golden Retriever puppy into my life a couple of years ago has been significant. She has brought me comfort with companionship and routine. But who knew later-life love would spring forth upon taking Mellie to dog training classes! Yes, there and at church I discovered Carol, a woman wonderfully suited as it turns out, not only to be our dog trainer but also my future wife! All this and more! At the first of the year I retired from work as a parish pastor, accepting an exciting new call to ministry in spiritual direction.

In out-of-the-way places of the heart I have journeyed through loss and grief, holding nothing back, learning to find ease in risk, waiting until I was ready to emerge. Grace sufficient I will continue to find myself in rhythm and at home here on Whidbey Island. My soul senses a new life that awaits me!

So, thank you for being that childhood friend who resurfaced just when I needed you for this leg of the journey. You have been especially kind receiving my letters graciously. And yes, God willing, Carol and I will look forward to visiting with you here on Whidbey and at your home in years to come.

Your childhood friend,

Jerry

Poems

Fresh Green Leaves

On a walk
through the wood
last night
in a grove of trees
I looked up
into a myriad of
fresh green leaves,
shimmering in
the late day sun

That's when I heard
a choir of angelic voices
with her smile
in every
glistening green face

No,
I wasn't over-medicated
simply touched
by the Spirit of
the living Lord

Divine beauty
sang
in a lonely moment
stirring up
hope and joy

Now Comes the Poet

I think I caught a glimpse
today
of a world
that is truly home

After scientists,
economists,
and every camp
of certitude
now comes the poet
evoking a different globe
a new song
a fresh self
a creative residence!

Sacred Cedar

Warm spring sun
covered by clouds,
my face wet in mist and rain
I walk
a few miles from home
to an ancient Cedar

She is increased by more than
500 seasons of
sorrow and joy,
hers a towering wisdom
of natural elements
in still, heightening awareness

A sacred Cedar's capacity to issue
life into air, soil, heart and soul
is equal to her vulnerability
before mighty winds
that send countless branch, trunk and needle
sailing to their death every year

In rain I lay eye and hand
on fragrant wood
feeling a surge of energy,
her root, deposit and sway
lifting Spirit heavenward,
my soul ablaze!

Visitor
(Kokopelli)

Maybe
our stretch of
sunny, warm weather
lured him to this
Pacific Northwest island

Maybe
he knew the change of season
here and in my heart
was ripe occasion for dance
to the sensual sounds and
magic of his music

I just know he came to visit
right here on Whidbey Island
and I am grateful
for Love's use of this lively legend
to express my wonder and delight

By a Sea of Grace

Whidbey Island was
like an out-of-way
place of the heart
three years ago,
my mind never thought
to wander here
where a beginning has
quietly been forming.

This lovely isle
waiting, waiting,
waiting until I was
ready to emerge,
is home
to a new song,
spirit awakened
I by a sea of grace
willing and able
to find peace in risk.

On this island
I am-
linked with family
encircled by friends,
accompanied by
a four-pawed heart,
and held in a woman's love.

Here and now
giving thanks
to the source
of my being
I live my song,
unfurled into the beauty
of a whole new beginning

The Dreamer in Me Asks

She saw it hanging
in the balance
with delicate flower-like wings
A butterfly
waiting, drying,
abandoning
the dreary, worm world
for blue sky, fresh breeze and...

Look, it's flying!

And the dreamer in me asks
Might I be
metamorphosed?
What need I leave behind?
What possibilities await
were I to give wing and
let go
of this
my current state?

New Wings

Out from the shadows
of loss and grief
Mine new wings
on wind of change

Life to flourish
sure to end,

Only to find
new life again

Dawn of Pentecost

All we
one tree
rooted and rained on
Reaching, reaching
inward, forward, upward
in manifestations of Divine
Drinking, drinking
of one Spirit
bearing fruit
for common good
Swaying, praying
in wind and wonder
abundantly alive!

Evergreen Island

From across the country
rolling into town
a family gathering
on Whidbey

Death of loved one
becoming sweet invitation
to a wide new world
of life together

Strange frontier afresh
stirring possibilities of late
on this evergreen island
in a salt water Sound

Outside Worship

Outside worship
among the trees
on this bright day
of memories,
I saw her
fly in the breeze
with countless
blades of greenery!

Her Smile

In the beauty of
wild daisies
there is intimacy
longing satisfied
for loved one gone,
divine assurance
of soul's wellbeing
her smile—
spring flowers
everywhere!

All Saints' Sunday

Our last trip to California
along a popular drive
just outside Carmel
there stood The Lone Cyprus,
hundreds of years old
atop a huge rock
far above
salty waves of the sea
constantly battering
the stones below

Still, for all the water
our eyes could see
only a trace of fresh rain
falls each year
on ancient roots of
The Lone Cyprus Tree

Yet, fog comes daily
leaving dew on the
tree branches,
drops falling gently
satisfying thirsty wood
with a source for green

This is All Saints' Sunday
a celebration of that
Great Cloud of Witnesses
that comes daily to
satisfy thirsty souls.

Peach, Limestone, and Green

She
is among them,
her living presence
leaving us
a deep drink,
washing tears away
helping satisfy each day
what we
thirst for most

Wave of Brightening

Days have begun to set
around our loss

Faith stirs a wave of
brightening

We rise
clothed in
vibrant colors of dawn

Wet Whidbey Dawn

I am night
were Love gone
on this cold,
wet Whidbey dawn

Day without sun
tree void of green
water's lofty blue
none

Yet,
in my soul's
deep, dark furrows
lies a dazzling inner
landscape

Heart of my heart
sings a love song
harvesting
tasty fruit

In spite
of the night
Love shines in the morn
and I am satisfied!

Holmes Harbor

Holmes Harbor
last night
like a sheet of glass
giving pause for
quiet mind,
calm heart,
home

Sound of Trains

There are times
I feel weak and wonder,
where is life going
and how will I manage to get there?

On the south end of Whidbey Island
along with the occasional sound
of the ferry horn, birds, coyote
and the wind through pine,
you can hear trains on the mainland
rolling along the water,
reminding me of those
in childhood that ran
along the Mississippi
with whistle and track clatter
echoing all day and night
off grand limestone bluffs

In Freeland I don't hear
in my ear
the sound of trains
with steady clatter on their tracks
but I feel the movement
of a glorious locomotive
in the depth of my being

Like the little engine that could
amidst commotion of
conflicting thoughts and feelings,
I hear the tiny whisper of

Jerry R. O'Neill

a mighty motor
moving me with steadfast rhythm
and unlimited power
toward a fullness of life,
assuring that what I imagine
I will realize
and what I desire
has already arrived

In this and every Freeland moment
is the thrill of adventure
living local, believing large

Thanksgiving

I'll have a piece of pumpkin pie
and ponder what I've learned
from this a year that's soon gone by
all given, gained and yearned

I'll harvest what's been loved and lost
give thanks for gifts it brought
and for the quiet way my Lord
brings near what soul has sought

Katie Next Door

Her name is Katie
Like her German accent
her simple life style offers
distinct articulation of values
good for the soul

With surgical precision
she cuts wood
and stacks it
to burn for heat
in the chilly, wet winter

She tends to her flowers,
fruit trees, and vegetables
and carefully mows
a large yard that stretches to
the shore of Cultus Bay

My neighbor lives
close to nature
grounded in the
rhythms and pleasures
of tide and season

She is teaching me
a depth of life
found in
the real places
to which we belong

Sensing Her Nearness

Today
I saw a robin
breathing
on the branch
of a fruit tree
in early spring
sunrise

For a brief moment
there were
two
and past them
beyond the tree
I saw robins
all around!

Whidbey Green

Earth remains soft
on Whidbey Island
Though days grow short
ocean waves
keep temps mild
well above
freezing

The ground into which
we placed the urn
containing Denise's ashes
was hard
knee deep in snow
on a bleak
midwinter day
in Minnesota

Oh, would we have had
a blanket to wrap
her remains
soft and green
like year-round
Whidbey fields

Instead
for warmth
we held each other
and as
golden light shown
on western skies

Peach, Limestone, and Green

        we listened
     to a foot-stompin'
       country song,
      sang a chorus
       about love
      and the taste
of southern fried chicken,
    and then we laughed,
     we laughed and
   we're still laughing
      in the face
         of
        winter

Acknowledgements

There are so many who have accompanied me on this journey through loss and grief over the past five years. Those for whom I'm especially grateful include my wife, Carol Gannaway, people on both sides of our family, our Minnesota family fellowship group, my childhood friend, Annie McGovern, Vikki Littleman, Rob and Kendra Setlow, the Staff and people of Trinity Lutheran Church in Freeland, Washington, other colleagues to include Chaplain Dave Bieniek, my spiritual director, Jamal Rahman, members and friends of faith communities in which I have had the privilege to live and serve, faculty and students at Seattle University's School of Theology and Ministry, Mary Knutson, Cathy Fanslow, and Jan Wright, Facebook friends, blog followers, a cloud of saints both here and on the other side, my cats Shell and Sable and my Golden Retriever Mellie Maple Whidbey.

Thanks to my sister, Peggy Driscoll for allowing me to use a number of her photos throughout the book.

I want to also thank Geri Giebel Chavis and John Fox for teaching me the principles of bibliotherapy and the value of reading and writing poetry for psycho-spiritual health and healing. They and others have encouraged me to publish these letters and poems.

Most of all, I thank Love Eternal for
Denise Carol (Peters) O'Neill
March 31, 1952-February 16, 2010

To this faithful, devoted, loving wife
and mother of our two daughters
Toby and Brooke,
who continues in the realm of Spirit
to inspire and enliven us,
I dedicate this book.

Other books by Jerry R. O'Neill

Out from the Shadows: Poetic Portraits of Faith

Whidbey Spiritual

Dr. O'Neill is founder of Whidbey Spiritual, an ecumenical and interfaith spiritual care and guidance practice serving people on Whidbey Island, Washington, throughout the Seattle area and beyond. He offers one-to-one and small group spiritual direction sessions, workshops and retreats promoting spiritual growth and wellbeing. To learn more go to
www.whidbeyspiritual.com

Blessed Assurance

That calmness
born of a deep certainty
of divine strength
widely available

Power of the holy
loving and guarding us
from all harm
and wrongdoing

Resting
again today
in communion with Divine
making this my intention:

That I may dwell
in a wellness of soul
and by the grace of God
live in quietness and peace

Made in the USA
Lexington, KY
20 July 2015